C000319115

Save a Seat for Me
Coping with Complicated Grief

by Erical

DORRANCE
PUBLISHING CO
EST. 1920
PITTSBURGH, PENNSYLVANIA 15238

Dorrance Publishing Co
585 Alpha Drive
Suite 103
Pittsburgh, PA 15238
Visit our website at *www.dorrancebookstore.com*

ISBN: 978-1-4809-3412-2
eISBN: 978-1-4809-3435-1

This book is dedicated to the memories of:
Elijah Jones, Velacita Monte Jones, Christina Jones,
and Torin Demarcus Jones.

"My Soul Has Been Anchored" is a Christian worship song that was recorded by Douglas Miller.

Letter from the Writers:

This song is a tribute to those having a difficult time coping with multiple losses. This song is reassurance that your loved ones will live on; however, remember this: Your loved one wants you to live on as well. You have a purpose, and in order to achieve that purpose you must move forward. There is no closure with death. Our family and friends who have passed live on through memories. Cherish them.

> Though the storms keep on raging in my life
> And sometimes it's hard to tell the night from day
> Still that hope that lies within is reassured
> As I keep my eyes upon the distant shore
> I know He'll lead me safely to that blessed place He
> has prepared
> But if the storm don't cease and if the winds keep on
> blowing in my life
> My soul has been anchored in the Lord.
> I realize that sometimes in this life,
> We're gonna be tossed be the waves and the currents
> that seem so fierce

But in the Word of God — I've got an anchor,
Oh, yes, I have, and it keeps me steadfast, unnam-
able, despite the tide
But if the storm don't cease and if the winds keep on
blowing in my life
My soul has been anchored in the Lord
My soul's been anchored
My soul's been anchored

My soul's been anchored
My soul's been anchored
The billows may roll, the breakers may dash
I will not stray because He holds me fast
Some darkless day that lies in the sky
I know it's all right 'cause Jesus is nigh
My soul's been anchored
My soul's been anchored
My soul's been anchored
My soul's been anchored
you crush me down but Jesus picks me up
He sticks right by me when the going gets tough
My soul's been anchored
My soul's been anchored
My soul's been anchored
My soul has been anchored in the Lord.

(Recorded by Douglas Miller)

"Ajax"

The foundation of this book was created when I lost my brother, Torin. His death inspired me to recruit the assistance of my sister Erical, who is a Special Nurse. . I needed the perspective insight from one of the youth in our family who has had to find coping mechanisms for each loss, and I chose my nephew Malik. He will graduate high school this year. Malik will also receive his Associate's Degree from Richard Bland College the same month. That he graduates High School.

Through the course of the following experiences, you will read about a family who has lost four family members within a two-year period. Each family member died in a different manner.

I have lost a wife to suicide. She shot herself in the head on February 25, 2012.

My father had a massive heart attack and died September 15, 2012, the day after my birthday.

My sister Velacita was murdered at her job by her abusive boyfriend, whom she finally found the strength and courage to leave on July 8, 2013.

My brother jumped off of a bridge into oncoming traffic and was struck by multiple vehicles. He died February 25, 2014; this was the two-year anniversary of my wife's suicide.

Our purpose is to give one person who is reading this book hope. You are not alone. We had to recognize and truly understand that we had to give all of the hurt, anger, loss, and pain over to our Higher Power (Adrian, Erical, and Malik).

I read the eloquent words of my nephew, and I decided that we would begin this book with his story. The children and young adults have a difficult time coping with death, much less multiple deaths. I've seen firsthand that in some cases their friends are unable to support them emotionally because they aren't equipped psychologically.

"Save a Seat for Me"
through the Eyes of Malik

As a member of the Jones and Tyler family, I wasn't really socially active with them. When I really reflect on my life, I learned that I shared very little memories with my family. I learned that throughout life the only true memories I held were when I was incapable of making my own decisions. As a result, I regret not getting involved in their lives socially. I wasn't able to receive the wisdom from my aunt (Christina), my grandfather (Elijah), my aunt (Velacita), and my uncle (Torin).

Even though I was not very socially active, as a child my family took plenty of pictures. Pictures of my life with my grandfather say a thousand words more than I can remember growing up. But as I look back at the pictures, I can say I had genuine memories of the great times I spent with my grandfather, my aunts and my uncles; at family functions we had after and routinely, such as birthdays, cookouts, family reunions, Christmas breakfast and Christmas dinners.

Though the winds are beneath me and the clouds look after me, I cherish my memories that take me through happiness, the trials I face to reach my errors, the mistakes I fix to please my era, the family bonding shared that was proven to increase my stability, to disguise my insecurities, to raise my infallibility. (Malik)

My grandfather (Elijah) was very wise. Most people would say the same for their grandparents. My grandfather didn't talk much. He used his actions to express what he had in mind. When he did talk, it would be something that would boggle your mind. There was never a time I spoke to him and it was a straightforward answer. In his sentences he would have secret messages that you would have to decode in order to know what he was saying.

The man I looked up to the most while expressing my feelings in this book—well, my uncle (Adrian) — is an inspiration to me. I would come to his house not to enjoy the neighborhood, the people in the neighborhood, or the fast-food restaurant that was down the street. I came to his house to spend quality time with him, his wife (Christina), who is now deceased, and his two children. I could remember the days when I would go over their house. It would be me and my older brother, and we would play "Jeopardy!" on the PlayStation 2. I was young, so I barely knew any of the answers. I only played because I had fast fingers. To be able to answer a question, you would have to buzz in by pressing the "X" button, and the first one to press it gets to answer first. My aunt would always choose me to be on her team while my uncle was left with my brother. The games would always end close. At Final Jeopardy, we would try to make it so that we beat them by only $1.

Everyone has their own trials and tribulations, while I just smile and have my own rehabilitation, living life without the truth of our creation, learning from my ancestors what they believe is the truth while I second guess my existence because of no proof, I dream of a world full of lust and treasure, but when I wake it's a life of cruelty and anxiety, fake and reality, violence and poverty, just what's supposed to come out of this world… I've been teased, I've been heartbroken,

I've been stabbed in the back, I've been flat out dropped from the highest peak to the ground, but I rise to my mound, overcoming the obstacles left to drown us in the life of depression and recession, I came to the conclusion that it's just a mess to sweat what drops from the rest. (Malik)

My aunt (Velacita) had many struggles in her life, none of which anyone knew about. Velacita was one to deal with her problems her way. She was strong. She has three children, two of whom are mentally challenged. My aunt was murdered, gunned down at work by her partner.

My aunt was never one to beat around the bush. We would have intense conversations about life. She never showed that she was hurting or in trouble, but I always could tell something wasn't right. There was nothing I could do. I miss her. I miss everyone who has passed away. I struggled every day to try to keep it together, and not express myself. I am struggling in this world right now trying to put the pieces of my empty life back together over and over still searching for something. I find myself expressing it in the wrong way not intentional just bad ways catch up to me to show me that I am not in control but Grace and Favor is what my family was built on in the church and I 've been running. I guess from being frustrated and upset with the man upstairs (GOD) for so long. Questioning how could he allow these incidents to happen to my family back to back and in a blink of and eye he took four important people from our family. I understand now "save a seat for me" because I have been at the door many close calls over the past few years. I am going to strive to overcome my hurt and talk more instead of putting it all in my music. I know now the help mom was sending me to was really for my good . I am going to try to reach out to her as well. I encourage anyone suffering in silence don't do it. Find a friend or a family member to talk to and release all the hurt and frustration and know that you are normal and it's healthy to cry. (Malik)

Erical

Look into my eyes and see if you could read me, does my ignorance deceive the blessings in which to cleanse me, until the end of today and the beginning of tomorrow to speak without a problem would be the end of my sorrows, is this the life worth living if it ends with a borrow, tell me how you decipher whom it is to follow, is it their appearance or the fancy clothes they wear or is it the overwhelming love that they claim to share? (Malik)

Chapter One
Christina

(Adrian) I was at work and had an epiphany. I realized that I had suffered the loss of four family members but I was in therapy, medicated, supported by my job and family (because the losses were so violent it couldn't be hidden), and supported spiritually by my church. I still struggle. I remember when the third death occurred; my sister Velacita was murdered at her job by an abusive boyfriend. She was the first of my siblings to pass. It was a searing pain. I was in therapy and still found myself walking out of the house, contemplating suicide myself.

My wife, Christina, all she had was me and an annual visit to a rehab to detox once a year. Somehow she was still able to keep a smile on her face while attempting to cope with severe depression.

I remember so vividly the guilt I felt for not being equipped to recognize what she was going through and not supporting her through it. It was too late....

(Adrian) I need two chicken fried steaks dropped for this next order. (The omelet cook handed me a spinach omelet.) What is this? Make it over.

I could tell she was angry. It was the third time she was making the same omelet for this order.

(Christina) (Slams the skillet down and turns to me): I got twelve more orders to make. What's wrong with it?!?

(Adrian) It's runny and we both know that it's gonna come back. So let's get it right the first time. Order up!

Four minutes went by, and she slid a platter with a perfect spinach omelet on it toward me.

(Adrian) Thank you.

(Christina) (Takes her chef's hat off and begins to walk out of the kitchen, sobbing.)

We were friends, but in the kitchen at work it was fierce during Sunday morning breakfast and we just had to get the job done. However, Christina seemed distracted lately. She was quiet but probably one of most intelligent people I have ever met. A true Beatles fanatic, she just raved about them.

(Adrian) (Looking around): Is she okay?

(Waitress) She just found out yesterday that her father was diagnosed with cirrhosis of the liver and it was in its late stages. He was dying.

Her father, Henning Andreasen, passed away eight days later. She was devastated; I didn't see her back at work for two weeks. It was obvious that she was still grieving, but she put on a strong outward appearance.

During the next few months, she and I became closer. It was as though she felt safe talking with me. She and I eventually parted ways after I left the restaurant a year later.

Six months later, after separating from my wife, I decided to look her up and I stopped by her home only to find out that her mom had recently passed from cancer. I had no idea that she was in love with me until she confessed this secret to me during our visit. Christina wasn't doing well herself....

I will never forget the condition of the home as she let me in to visit. I've never been one to judge a friend, but I knew she needed support not criticism. The only thing that gave her the strength and will to get up each day was her son, Klaus. Her son was there and they were lying on the sofa in the living room, enjoying each other's company while watching a television show.

She invited me to spend the night, and it was nice catching up with her. When I woke the next morning, I wanted to fix them breakfast. I walked into the kitchen and opened the fridge, and 90 percent of the food was spoiled. I stayed the next few weeks and cleaned her home and spent time with Klaus while she binge drank. She needed a friend to help and support her, not someone to judge her. She was suffering from the loss of both parents in less than two years. I felt at this point we needed each other, and I believed she felt the same. A few weeks later, after her son went to school, we had a conversation one afternoon....

(Christina) I wondered what happened to you. Has everything been okay?

(Adrian) Things just weren't working out. We just grew apart. I loved my wife and missed my children, but the relationship just wasn't healthy.

(Christina) I totally understand. I had to leave Mason; he was just too abusive. The last straw was when he threw my son across the room. He was beating me up, too, so I just couldn't take the chance on my child being physically abused also.

(Adrian) (I could see the pain in her eyes.) I missed you. Hey, remember when we went to eat at that sushi place over by La Jolla Coves?

(Christina) (Laughs): What I remember is that your eyes were tearing on that wasabi. I missed you, too.

She reached over to wrap her arms around me and gave me a soft

3

kiss on my lips. We just looked into each other's eyes. We both knew right then our lives would be inseparable.

Klaus and my son, Aric, spent time together with me, and all we did was go to McDonald's and "Family Fun Center." They both had enough going on in their lives, and Christina wanted them to just enjoy being children, if only for the day.

She had inherited money from her mother's passing away. The year was 1997, and we decided that after Klaus' school year was complete we would relocate to Maryland. It was hard for me to leave my children and move. It was going to be difficult for her to leave because she only had one living sibling left, who was her brother Johnnie. She loved him.

We drove cross country, and we talked about everything in our lives. Her drinking had subsided, and she was getting healthy. I was excited when we entered the state of Virginia. My first stop was at my home in Prince George, Virginia.

The visit was bittersweet; my father had remarried, and because Christina and I weren't married he wasn't going to allow us to stay in the home that I grew up in. We were tired, but my father and her brother gave us the same look.... She was European, and I was African-American. When Christina and I looked at each other, we saw two human beings.

(Adrian) Let's go, Chris.

Once we were in the moving van, I looked over at her.

(Adrian) The next stop we make is going to be at our home in Maryland.

We talked a lot about her family during the rest of the trip. She loved her father so very much. It was clear that the relationship with her mother was strained. I think she felt as though she couldn't measure up to the person her mother wanted her to become. Her father loved her unconditionally, and his personality was free spirited and she missed that about him. It was difficult for her to move on with both parents deceased because she never felt as though she was successful. She wanted her mother to say she was proud of her. Yet Christina's mother criticized her and gave Johnnie accolades for underachieving. She was hurt by the favoritism. This caused a rift between her and Johnnie, and sadly the division of the inheritance didn't bring them closer. But she always talked about her brother in an endearing manner. She really wanted to mend their relationship. She just didn't know how....

(Christina) How far is Maryland from here?

(Adrian) It's not far, four hours maybe. How soon is Joshua joining us? He seemed excited about the move.

(Christina) I think the new start is what he needs right now.

Joshua arrived a month later and was excelling in school. He made friends quickly and seemed to be adjusting well to the move. It was good to see both of them happy. They loved each other so much.

Over the course of the next six months, the rent, which was paid in advance, had been exhausted and I had just got a job as a grocery clerk. It was something different, and we needed income to take care of our home. I remember coming home late in the evening after work and sitting in the living room eating my dinner when Christina sat down beside me to tell me she was pregnant. When I heard the news, I felt overwhelmed but I couldn't tell her. She trusted me to make sure we were safe and our family was provided for.

(Adrian) Honey, I need some help with the finances. We can't make ends meet on what I am bringing home from the store. I need you to get a part-time job.

I was concerned because she was drinking boxes of wine. I always found empty Franzia boxes in different places in our home. I was concerned about the amount of alcohol she was ingesting daily. I just wanted her healthy during this pregnancy. I didn't want her over-

5

whelmed, and her happiness meant the world to me. I had to find a way to show her how I felt without coming across as judgmental. We talked about everything, and I didn't want our communication to suffer or cease.

(Christina) I will start looking next week.

Two weeks later, she was hired at the corner liquor store. I thought to myself, *this cannot be happening*. I was happy that this job didn't work out. She got a job as a waitress not long afterward. It was too much on her back, and I couldn't risk her injuring herself or the baby, so I asked her to quit and stay home. She was about three months along at this time, and I was doing pretty well at my new job. She was still drinking, and my concern was concentrated on Joshua's wellbeing as well. He needed his mother's nurturing at such a young age. She was an awesome mother. I believe she learned how to love her children from her own mother's mistakes.

(Joshua) Mom! The mailman is here. He says you have to sign for a package.

(Christina) Coming.... (She notices the envelope has a San Diego County Court address on it as she signs for it.)

She opened the package and began to briefly read over the enclosed papers. She sat down, and her expression turned to sadness; Joshua's father was petitioning the court for custody citing that she was an unfit mother....

(Adrian) Honey, you know this is about our relationship, the expecting of our child, and the obvious, his refusal to support his child financially. It has nothing to do with your ability to care for Joshua. After all, you've been doing it alone for all these years.

(Christina) I know that, but just the thought of Joshua having to fend for himself with his father scares me. He won't even talk to me when I call to let him know how the child is doing.

(Adrian) Chris, that's all you can do. We can't control everything.

Maybe he needs to see for himself what type of father he has. This way he can see from his own experience instead of what others may try and say of his father.

(Christina) (Sobbing softly): Adrian, I love him so much.

(Adrian) I am so sorry this is happening. (I reached over and just held her.)

I had never seen her look as devastated and so defeated. I just didn't have the words to fix this situation. Her spirit was temporarily broken, and I was helpless in mending the pain. I needed to pray and give it over to my higher power. In hindsight, I realize my first mistake was to think that I could fix the turmoil going on in her life.

The hearing was held in San Diego, California, four months later, and due to our financial circumstances she was unable to appear in person. Christina did write a letter to the courts and was there via telephone. When it was all over, Mason was awarded custody.

I had been finding empty Franzia wine boxes hidden in the pantry and laundry room. I needed to address her binge drinking but not come across to critical. I knew she was fragile because of the recent loss of Joshua to his father, but her health and the baby's health were still at risk if this behavior continued. The baby was due within the next couple weeks....

(Adrian) After getting off from work, I heard cooking in the kitchen. I noticed a large cup sitting to the side on the counter. Chris, if you keep this up, the baby's amniotic fluid is going to be wine.

(Christina) (Either ignores my comment or sidesteps it): Dinner's almost ready. How was your day?

(Adrian) Did you hear what I just said? Look, I know you're going through a lot, but how are you going to feel if there are complications with the baby?

(Christina) Okay, I promise to rein it in. I just....

(Adrian) (I interrupted her): You're not in this alone. We will get through this together. I just need you to take better care of you.

The baby arrived a week early, but she was healthy and as beautiful as her mother. We named her McClaine. McClaine's arrival saved her mother's life. It gave her purpose to want to curb her drinking and live for her daughter. Christina and I married a year later. Things were looking good for us.

After six years in Maryland, we decided it was time to move to Virginia. Most of my siblings were still there, and it was important that a close relationship was developed with Christina and my family. She only had her brother as immediate family left in the United States, and she was trying desperately to mend their relationship. I could tell from their conversations lately that Johnnie was making an effort with her.

It was difficult leaving Maryland because I had worked my way up from a store clerk to a floor manager making a decent salary. I realized it wasn't about me. What was my wife and child to do should something unforeseen happen to me and we were out of state?

It was decided and we made the move on faith to Virginia.

After two months in Virginia, I was hired on with the greatest retailer on the planet earth as an area floor manager. Two days after finalizing my contract with my new corporate job, I received more great news from my wife. She was pregnant again, and we were expecting a baby boy. I was ecstatic from the news. I had two wonderful sons in San Diego, but due to the divorce I was rarely able to spend quality time with them due to the distance we were apart. I loved both of my sons dearly, Duant'e and Dimitri. I always made time to either visit with them or talk on the phone with them, and I never missed a birthday. I learned with my children that if you say you're going to do something with or for them, you have to follow through. No excuses and no lying. Children remember and they will lose faith and trust if you are inconsistent or never available for them.

We had just gotten settled into our new home; however, six months later, just when our life as a family was making a turn for the better, we received more devastating news....

(Christina) (Phone rings): Hello?

(Ashley, Johnnie's daughter) Hi, Aunt Christina.

(Christina) Ashley, you don't sound well. Is everything okay?

(Ashley) (Breaks down crying): My father was found unresponsive this morning at his home. He's dead!

(Christina) What! (Stands up and flips over her chair over) How?

(Ashley) At this point, we are unsure.

(Christina) I'm going to see what I can do to help support you. I need you to know that I love you and I am here for you. Can I call you back at this number?

(Ashley) Yes, this is my number. I'll be okay, but it just hurts. I feel so emotionally drained. Can I talk to you later?

(Christina) Of course, sweetie. I love you.

(Ashley) I love you, too. I will talk with you later.

I was in our living area when I had overheard this conversation. I immediately ran over to take her into our room. I had to comfort her; I loved her much and she was hurting. She was sobbed so long into my chest, which my shirt was drenched with her tears. I started to pray to God to heal my family.

I knew that she had struggled to get her alcohol usage under control. Even now it hadn't dawned on me that my wife was attempting to cope with severe depression and she needed professional help. I thought she was just abusing alcohol.

The culmination of the three deaths—her father, mother, brother, and loss of her son to his father, all within a period of eight years—would eventually become overwhelming. However, with the birth of our son arriving within the month, her focus was on staying healthy to the best of her ability.

She still drank but not even close to the amount she had drank with McClaine. The baby was born in September, and we named him Deican. Everything was going fine until December came, and I was reminded that this was the month that her father had passed.

She drank uncontrollably from this period on. She began to neglect our children, the condition of the home began to suffer, and dinner wasn't getting cooked regularly.

Then the unthinkable happened. While I was at work, she attempted to shoot herself but the gun misfired.... (This was the first sign that she was serious about ending her life. I didn't recognize it because I didn't see my future without her. So I dismissed this incident....)

What's interesting is that after the attempted suicide, Chris and I never discussed it. In my mind, I believed if there was something she wanted to talk about that was troubling her she would eventually come to me and confide in me.

The problem with this was after a few weeks of the isolation and neglect of our home and children; I got frustrated and confronted her with what I expected for our household.

She was always home and my concern, as ill-fated as it may seem, was "If you're going to be a functional alcoholic, then you have responsibilities, and first and foremost is the perception that our children have of their mother." Children are so dismissive of our faults because they want to see their parents as role models and their protectors. They intentionally neglect to see the flaws until they have been hurt by the parent.

I never wanted to come across as a dictator to my wife because she had been accustomed to that all of her life, but she needed someone who could reason with her to the point that she would accept responsibility for her actions.

(Adrian) Honey, our corporate dinner is the first week in January. We had a really nice time last year.

(Christina) What should I wear?

(Adrian) Baby, I'm sorry, but I'm not taking you this year. I can't; your drinking has become excessive and I love you. It's not about you embarrassing me, but I love you. I can't take the chance on you humiliating yourself. That was the end of that conversation....

Three months later, I was over visiting my brother-and-law James when I received a phone call from the state police that there was an accident involving my wife and children....

(State Police) Sir, do you know a Christina Jones?

(Adrian) Yes, I do. She is my wife. What is this about?

(State Police) Sir, we need you to come to Route 35 by the overpass near the Walmart storage facility as soon as possible.

(Adrian) I'm on my way.

I was in a panic, and I was unsure of what the circumstances were going to be that I was about to walk into....

When I arrived to the scene, I noticed there were three troopers at the scene. I saw my wife over to the side. Our children were alive and safe, but the vehicle was totaled. It had been t-boned by a tow truck. That didn't matter to me because my family was alive and that was the major concern to me. I exited my vehicle and began to walk over to the scene, when I was approached by an officer....

(Trooper) Sir, are you Adrian?

(Adrian) Yes, sir, I'm Adrian. This is my family. Is everyone okay?

(Trooper) Everyone is fine. I am concerned about your wife. Is she a heavy drinker?

I was unsure of how to answer because I wanted to protect my wife. But as I looked over in her direction, I realized she was unable to keep her balance but the dead giveaway was her eyes. I could tell if she was intoxicated just from the condition of her eyes. I didn't have to smell the alcohol. She was the love of my life, and I knew her body and mannerisms. She was drunk.

Erical

(Adrian) Sir, I need you to arrest my wife. I'm concerned about her, and she needs a reality check that there are consequences. But most of all, I'm fearful that my wife is going to hurt herself or someone else if she chooses to drink and drive again in this condition.

Once Christina was released from jail the next day, I admitted her into Poplar Springs. It was a detoxification center, along with group therapy. My failure was I was more concerned about detoxing the alcohol from her body instead of the primary focus being on healing her pain from the losses in her life. She needed coping skills to deal with her family's passing and the loss of her son to Mason.

Over the course of the next few months, Christina's drinking subsided. She entered an ASAP program, and it seemed as though she was doing much better. Deican's birthday was held at Chuck E. Cheese's. She played the perfect mother and hostess. We didn't get to have the traditional Thanksgiving dinner because I worked this year at my job. My job had started Dot Com to increase competition with Amazon, and I was the manager on duty through this process.

December came quickly, and the bottom fell out from under our family. Christina's fathers passing hit her with such force, she was unable to recover. The love she had for him as a father and protector wasn't obvious then but in hindsight....

The family is getting prepared for Sunday morning service at first Baptist Church West Petersburg.

(McClaine) Dad, I have been talking to Mom about getting baptized.

(Adrian) That's great. How is it going?

(McClaine) I'm not sure, but she said she was thinking about it.

(Adrian) It's a huge step and a lifelong commitment to GOD. We're talking eternal life here.

(McClaine) Dad, I know. I'm going to take Deican to the car and wait for you guys.

All I could do was smile.

(Adrian) Okay, we will be there shortly.

I headed toward the bathroom to hurry my wife along.

(Adrian) Chris, the kids are waiting for us.

(Christina) I'm ready.

(Adrian) You look kind of sexy for church.

(Christina) (Smiles). Shut up, let's go.

When the pastor had finished his sermon, he asked if anyone wanted to give their life to GOD. My wife stood up and walked toward the front of the church. I remember walking up to support her and I reached over and hugged her tightly....

(Adrian) (I whispered in her ear): I love you. Honey, you just saved our marriage.

The baptism happened after the New Year, and the next few days were a reminder of how precious our marriage was to both of us. However, I'm unsure what transpired, but my wife's alcohol abuse and depression went into a tailspin and was out of control....

(McClaine) Dad, Mom is passed out at the neighbor's house across the street.

She said it so matter–of–fact like...with no emotion.... She was embarrassed, but she carried her pride well. McClaine loved her mother, but she was unaware of how to help her through her pain. McClaine's concern came out in angry outburst toward her mother. My daughter was frustrated, and once again I didn't know how to fix this disease that was tearing our family apart. My eleven-year-old daughter was playing grown-up to her mother and baby brother without my realizing it was happening.

(Adrian) 'Claine, stay here with Deican. I'll be right back.

I drove across the street and placed my wife in the vehicle and drove her home. I carried her to our room and placed her in bed to sleep off the intoxication.

The following six weeks were brutal. Her drinking intensified to the point I just didn't come home after work until it was time for me to get the children off to school in the morning. I just couldn't take seeing her like this anymore. Then that day, February 25, came....

It was about 10 P.M., and I was busy at work when I received a call from Christina. I remember being upset and telling her unless she got help I was taking our children and leaving her. What was I thinking to say such cruel words to the mother of my children? She had already lost a father, mother, brother, and her firstborn child to his father. We were all she had left....

(Christina) (Dials my ex-wife and when she answers the phone she calmly begins to speak): Sorry to bother you, but are you busy?

(Leta) No, I'm not busy. Is everything okay?

(Christina) Of course, everything is fine. I just wanted to ask a favor of you.

(Leta) Sure, what is it?

(Christina) Should something happen to me, would you please take care of my McClaine and Deican?

(Leta) Absolutely, as long as you promise to take care of Duant'e, Adria, and Dimitri if something should happen to me.

My wife waited till the children went to sleep and wrote a suicide note. In the letter she said that she loved the children and we would be better off without her.

When I arrived home at 3 A.M., I found that letter on our bed. I first checked our closet where we kept a small caliber handgun for protection. It was missing. I found myself frantically searching the house looking for her and could not locate her. I was praying that she had taken a walk and would be returning home soon, but I kept looking for her. I went outside and walked out of our patio door to the backyard. I found my wife lying on the ground. She had shot herself in the head. I knelt down beside her and felt her face. She was so cold. In my hysteria, I screamed for my neighbors to help me. I was so empty. I needed her to wake up. She was gone.

Adrian dials his sister and with and emotional loud tone he speaks: (Erical) Christina is hurt! Cracking voice noted, she is hurt...

Erical (Adrian) I am on my way. With the sound of worry in my voice, I jump up out the bed. Trying to make sense of what I might need, searching for my medical bag. I hear my husband James, (Erical) slow down you can't drive like that, we will talk on the way... Erical speaking to my oldest son please keep the doors locked, and the alarm on we will be back shortly. It was the longest drive ever for me. When we arrived there were police lights and Lights from Ambulances. I saw my brother Adrian sitting on his step with a friend comforting him. I remember walking up to him.

Erical (Adrian) where is Chrissy? I bought my medical bag to fix her. Where did she get hurt at? Tell me something? Somebody anybody we are losing time... EMT looked over at me and said I am sorry to tell you this, she is gone. I was frozen in time. I hugged my brother Adrian tightly as tears fell then I remembered.

Erical (Adrian) where are the kids? I need to see them and make sure they were ok. They were across the street at a neighbor house with the look of confusion on their face.

If I could offer any words of advice to someone contemplating suicide, it would be this: "Your life may seem as though it has no purpose just for this moment, but I encourage you to fight to stay alive one more day. The ones who love you are not aware of how to heal your pain, but they will struggle with your passing should you choose to take your life" (Adrian Jones, 2014).

Christina's suicide affected everyone close to her, and each person felt a sting of personal guilt that they were unable to prevent her death.

"Professional treatment and involvement in re-covery can make a significant positive impact on

clients and their families in managing the disorders and improving the quality of life. There are many effective treatments for depression including interpersonal psychotherapy, cognitive behavioral therapy, and supportive counseling; anti-depressant medications; and electroconvulsive therapy (ECT). There are also many effective treatments for addiction including behavioral therapies and counseling, and sometimes, the use of medications" (Dennis C. Daley, Ph.D., 2000).

Support Groups

- National Depressive & Manic-Depressive Association: www.ndmda.org; (800) 826-3632
- National Foundation for Depressive Illness, Inc.: www.depression.org; (800) 239-1265
- Dual Recovery Anonymous (DRA): www.dualrecovery.org; (888) 869-9230
- Alcohol Hotline: (800) 331-2900
- Al-Anon for Families of Alcoholics: (800) 344-2666
- Alcohol and Drug Helpline: (800) 821-4357
- Alcohol Treatment Referral Hotline: (800) 252-6465
- National Council on Alcoholism and Drug Dependence Hope line: (800) 622-2255
- Teen Help Adolescent Resources: (800) 840-5704

If you're suicidal, we recommend contacting the National Suicide Prevention Lifeline toll-free at 800-273-8255.

Chapter Two
Torin

"Happy are the mild-tempered ones, since they will inherit the earth." —Matthew 5:5

My father was in the Navy during Vietnam, and my mother was a housekeeper at the time of my birth. I was raised by my grandparents, Big Daddy and Big Mama, James and Nolie Parham. They kept me until it was time for me to go home to my parents. My brother was three years behind me in age, and as I think back on our growing up as kids he was always in my shadows. I was the big brother, and he was tagging along. The interesting thing about my little brother was he was always mad. He was just mean.

I remember when I was twelve years old and it was a school night....

(Adrian) (After I lie down in bed, my brother crawls over Me.): Torin, why are you in my bed? You know you have the top bunk! The bed isn't big enough for us both.

(Torin) I don't want to sleep up there tonight.

(Adrian) Why?

(Torin) (He doesn't bother to answer…rolls over.)

It seemed like an hour had passed after I had fell asleep when I felt a punch in the face. I knew what it was because it wasn't the first time that he had hit me in the face while we were sleeping. Torin had a habit of stepping across the line when we were growing up because he was just mean.

I must apologize to you, the reader. He was my only brother, and I cannot write about our relationship and his demise at this time.

Four months had gone by, and I would try and continue. During the three months that I stepped back to regroup, I learned that healing is a process. I still have only shed one tear for my brother. We weren't twins, but he was my only brother.

Sometimes being a brother is even better than being a superhero. It was nice growing up with someone like you—someone to lean on, someone to count on, someone to tell on! He was my most beloved friend and my bitterest rival, my confidant and my betrayer, my sustainer and my dependent, and scariest of all, my equal. I don't believe an accident of birth makes people sisters or brothers. It makes them siblings, gives them mutuality of parentage. Sisterhood and brotherhood is a condition people have to work at. There was a little boy inside the man who was my brother.... Oh, how I hated that little boy; how I loved him, too. (Adrian)(Erical) he was my confidant and my friend.

Over the course of time, it became evident to me that we were not just brothers but confidants as well. We talked about everything. Once he graduated high school, he flew out to Oceanside, California, to visit me. He was young, and he spent most of that time chasing women and running the streets. I will never forget the phone call that I received early one morning saying:

(Tom) Adrian, you have to come get your brother because some ESE's are looking to hurt him.

Once I found him and got him to safety, I put him on the next thing smoking out of California with a reminder that he was not to come back. This wasn't because I didn't want to see him but rather I wasn't prepared to lose my brother to foolishness....

Over the next five years, we touched base long distance just to check on one another. During that period he had met a woman by the name of Ann. Eventually they would have two children, Tinesha and Torin Jr.

He called me when his son was born....

(Adrian) Hello?

(Torin) What's up, bro?

(Adrian) Hey, man, how are things?

(Torin) You know what, I'm doing well. I have a newborn son now.

(Adrian) What! Man, I'm happy for you. I guess now you got to slow your roll and take care of home. All that running the streets is over, you know.

(Torin) Yeah, I know. I work for a trucking company that makes deliveries out of state. I love it, the money is good. I just hate being away from my children.

(Adrian) That's called sacrifice. I'm proud of you, man. Look, I'm moving to Baltimore in a few years. Just keep that in mind. I will be close to home, just not home. I'm not ready.

(Torin) I understand not wanting to come home right now. Nothing has changed so, well, you know.

I moved to Baltimore with my future wife, Christina, two years later and remember coming home and my wife saying:

(Christina) Honey, Torin called and said he was passing through and wanted to see you.

(Adrian) Thanks, Chris. Did he leave a number?

(Christina) As a matter of fact, he did. I also gave him our address. The number is on the hutch.

(Adrian) Thanks.

I called the number, and my brother picked up and after speaking for a few minutes we decided to meet at a restaurant called Barragan's for lunch.

When my brother showed up, he had that unique smile that was soft and genuine, much like our mother. He was in good spirits, and that alone made me happy. I spent much of my life concerned about him just because he was my only brother. I loved this kid. He gave so much and took virtually nothing in return if anything. His heart was pure. I adored him.

(Torin) What's up, old man?

We embraced. I just missed this guy.

(Adrian) How's home? It's probably still boring as ever.

(Laughing together....)

(Torin) I still have my time fishing. It's my peace of mind. Hey, did I ever tell you that story of how me and Willie shot killed a pig with a BB gun when we were, I guess, maybe thirteen years old?

(Adrian) No, but you know, I don't believe you can get in trouble for that today. You actually killed a pig with a BB gun? Wow, I'm sure Big Daddy probably tore you a new one for killing one of his farm animals. (I laughed.)

Our food arrived, and we continued to reminisce about our childhood. It was really nice just spending adult time with my brother. He had grown up and was maturing into a great dad and a responsible adult. He was proud of his accomplishments, and I was proud of him.

It couldn't have been more than two years later....

I will never forget the night that my wife and I drove from Maryland to Virginia to visit our family. Torin's children's mom was strung out on drugs, causing my brother all kinds of grief. It angered me to the point that I went to their home and told her what I really thought of her. It was devastating to see the hurt she was putting on him.

(Adrian) Bro, you got to think of your children's welfare. Annette's not ready.

(Torin) I love her, though, man. But I know you're right. I'm already overlooking the money she is stealing out of my wallet while I'm asleep and having other men driving my car. I can't take the kids from her. She's their mother.

(Adrian) Wrong, she is their mom but she isn't being a mother. Torin, you can't drink this away either, you know. That's another avenue that she is using against you. Once you're incapacitated, she takes advantage of you. Come on, man.

(Torin) I know....

When he said, "I know," I had to leave it alone. He had been hurt enough.

He wasn't perfect, but neither was I. He wasn't a self-centered, egotistical individual. My brother's biggest problem was not balancing his inner circle. He had to be pushed to the edge to finally say ENOUGH to those negatively affecting his children's future! Their mom....

"Throughout his years of adulthood he's been tormented by many, even his ex-wife and current wife. His ex-left he stranded with two children. My uncle (Torin) was already mentally unstable from previous situations. My uncle and I didn't talk much to each other but, from looking into his eyes you could see the pain he was going through. He tried to drink away his problems. Torin portrayed himself as a joyful, strong, kindhearted person. My uncle was also one to talk straightforward. He didn't sugarcoat any discussion. He was the type of person to mean what he says and say what he means" (Malik Tyler)

James 1:2-4: Consider it pure joy, my brothers and sisters, whenever you face trials of many kinds, because you know that the testing of your faith produces perseverance. Let perseverance

**finish its work so that you may be mature and
complete, not lacking anything.**

Over the course of the next two years, three things transpired. My
brother was pushed deliberately down a flight of stairs and broke his
leg. He had to have pins put in it in order to walk. This did not make
any sense to me because this was the same individual who had no
problem punching me in the face as a child.

The second thing was that Torin called me to see if it was okay
with Christina if he and the kids moved to Maryland and lived with
us until his leg healed. I was ecstatic and Christina was happy to have
the company. He moved in with us, and after a school year he decided
he had healed his body to the point of moving on. It was sad to see
him go....

The third thing that happened was me and my wife decided it was
time to move to Virginia. It was important that she developed a relationship with my siblings and our daughter was close to her cousins.
Once we were situated and moved in, my brother had moved back into
town from North Carolina; Started back driving routes out of town,
trusting Ann to be able to care for their children while he was away,
he had tried to reconcile with the children's mom and once again,
things didn't work out. He loved that woman. But she loved the drugs
more. It was midnight on a summer night a knock on the door.

Social Worker (are you Erical?) yes I am. Everything ok. As she
stand there with a pretty little 3 year old girl on one side and a scared
1 1/2/ year old little boy on the other side. Social Worker: I bring
them here because you were the next point of contact listed and to
keep the children out of foster care I wanted to see if you wanted to
care for them first. You see we found them wondering and walking
down by a swamp searching for their mother who said she was just
going to the store but that had been over several hours. My brother

was notified, and he was not happy about the situation. We went to court several times. Their mothers' rights were terminated and their father was granted joint custody. We worked together one day : at a time being a leader, a provider and protector for his children. We were able to show the courts how determined and ready he was to take on being a full-time father to his children. I was so proud of him. He needed a place to stay with the children, and my door was always open to him. He was there maybe three weeks before he had found a place and moved out. He was proud. He didn't like imposing, and he was a self-made man. It couldn't have been more than two months later and he had met a woman by the name of Delilah....

> **"If my people, which are called by my name,**
> **shall humble themselves, and pray, and seek my**
> **face, and turn from their wicked ways; then will**
> **I hear from heaven, and will forgive their sin,**
> **and will heal their land." (2 Chronicles 7:14)**

Once Torin and Delilah married, things appear to be really good the first year. I was so happy for him. My brother had a way of putting on a good face in the midst of troubling times. After that year passed, all things seemed to fall apart in my brother's life.

His thirteen-year-old daughter was molested by Delilah's sons, and his son was being bullied by one of the same individuals. My brother decided to give custody back to our sisters in order to protect them, while the authorities investigated the allegations of molestation in the case....

I will never forget the day that I drove him to social service to complete the paperwork....

(Adrian) (While we are sitting in the vehicle outside of social service): Torin, I know this is a stupid question, but are you okay?

(Torin) (Inhales the cigarette he is smoking and turns to blow the smoke out of the window. He turns to Me.): There is too much grief in that house, and my babies have been through enough as it is. I can no longer put them in that position. I have to protect them.

(He opens the door the car and exits, but before he walks off to the building he turns around just to say):

Thank you.

(Adrian) I'm your brother. Who else is going to put up with you? But you're welcome.

Torin entered into the social service building to finalize the paperwork for transfer of custody to our sisters. When he returned to the vehicle, he opened the door and sat down.

(Adrian) (I didn't pull off right away because I could see the pain on his face.) You did the right thing, bro. are you going to be okay?

(Torin) (Tears begin to stream down the side of his face. His crying goes into a wail filled with so much sorrow, hurt and pain emanating from his body.)

Through the course of my brother's adult life, he battled alcoholism and depression. His drink of choice was Black Velvet. It was an inexpensive whiskey, and he drank it straight. He wasn't the mean kid punching me in the face when we were kids but a man who had women in his life who broke his spirit and left him feeling alone in a crowded room.

> "Why love if losing hurts so much? We love to know
> that we are not alone."~ C.S. Lewis

Two weeks later, my brother stopped by my house after he had gotten off work.

(Torin) (Walks in the house and grabs my son, Dei'can_: Hey, Champ!

(Dei'can) Hi, Uncle Torin....

(Torin) When you going to come over and watch some television with me?

Torin loved Deican's company. I believe for two reasons. One, he was able to go to his room, shut the door, and watch his western movies. He loved westerns as much as our father did when we were growing up. Two, he could watch them in peace without being badgered by Delilah.

(Adrian) (I stop what I am doing and turn to him as Dei'can goes outside to play with his friends.): What you been up to?

(Torin) (He stands up and goes over to the hutch and begins to pour himself a drink): You know, my kids are gone and all she does is trying and find ways to blame my children for her son's mistakes. I can't take much more her calling me worthless and a drunk. (His phone begins to ring. He turns it off.)

(Adrian) When was the last time you went to church, man? You're trying to fix problems that only your Higher Power has the ability to do.

I didn't want to tell him that I saw his wife at a motel a couple days earlier. Why would I cause him more grief? I just wished he would leave her. He was welcomed at my house, and he found refuge there periodically until she rang his cellphone so much he had to turn it off. The problem wasn't that she was calling to see if he was but to just harass him.

(Torin) I haven't been in a while. I know where you're going with this, and I hear you.

I knew he was just trying to shut me up, and I obliged....

(Adrian) I heard you moved over by Cita. How is that going?

Cita (Velacita) was our sister.

(Torin) The move is done. I just have to get my CDL reinstated so I can get some real money coming in.

(Adrian) Let me guess, you got a house full of her convict sons living with you?

(Torin) (Laughs): Just two, but she really doesn't want them there.

(Adrian) Man, how is it you find yourself involved with some of the most dysfunctional people? I know we got problems, but the ones you choose to be involved with see dysfunction as their comfort zone.

(Torin) Yeah, I know…. (He just smiles and finishes his drink before saying goodbye to the children and heading back home.)

It was always good to see my brother. I took a special delight in seeing him. He was my true best friend. I knew that whatever we said between each other stayed between us.

My wife, Christina, and Torin were really close, and I knew her passing had affected him as much as it had me. After all, he and his children had lived with us often.

It wasn't even a week later I received a call that I needed to rush over to my brother's home because he had tried to commit suicide…

When I arrived, my brother was sitting on his sofa with his head in his hands. I asked his wife what had happened, and she described that he had a taken a belt and put it around his neck and tried to kill himself.

I remind you that I had already suffered the loss of my wife, and this particular situation worried me but also infuriated me. I was blunt and to the point with my brother.

(Adrian) What are you thinking!? You're my only brother. Did you think that choking yourself out with a belt was going to kill you? You may have passed out, but that was about all that would happen…

(Torin) (Lifts his head and looks me in the eyes but says nothing. I see sadness.)

The paramedics walk through the door, and I leave because I knew they would take him for evaluation at this point. I failed to see how broken he was. Even at this time. I loved him so much, and the thought of losing him would have been beyond devastating for me.

It was March 2013, and I transferred within my company to San Diego, California. My brother still hadn't gotten his CDL reinstated when I left, and he was still going through the turmoil of being in a hostile environment.

I knew when I left through his experience that men can be emotionally abused as well as women. It wasn't that he couldn't fight back with mean words or physical measures, but he was better than that as a human being.

(Erical) (June 2013 calls me to tell me that Torin moved out from Delilah's home and is living with Cita.)

(Adrian) That is great to hear. How is he doing?

(Erical) Well, you know your brother.

(Adrian) Erical, he was losing his will to live at that house. I'm glad he is with Cita. At least he is safe and can finally get some peace and quiet.

It is a month later, July 08, 2013, I receive a call that my sister Cita has been shot and killed by her estranged boyfriend at her job.

Torin eventually moves back in with his abusive wife, Delilah, after our sister is laid to rest. So my brother Adrian had thought: but Torin was hurting silently for so many reasons just like me now but speaking of Torin right now he would come through our decease sisters window and camp out there because he missed her so much. He was still in shock at the beginning then denial and finally, acceptance but never did he grieve for her that came months later.

Erical (Torin) I am going to leave this mattress here for you stay as long as you like for your sanity., as I am packing up my decease sisters home.

Torin (Erical) are you busy?

Erical (Torin) not for you, what's up?

Torin Paused: I wanted to know if you can come and get me

Erical I'll be right there

Knock -, knock the door was unlocked and he was in his bedroom sitting on his bed with tears in his eyes. I could see down the hall where there was frozen meat destroyed all over the floor from the freezer. I knew then it was not a safe place for my brother.

Erical (Torin) what happened

Torin looked up at me and he said "Do you see that white door there? I replied yes, noticing that the lock on the door was broke.

Torin "that's all I had was my door and she took that from me" and I knew then he was broken and hurt

Erical (Tell me what you need to pack up) let's take a couple sets of work clothes and shoes Your tools, your glucometer, cologne, hygiene stuff, and your wallet the rest is a later date if needed and we left I took him home with me. He slept peaceful no appetite when he woke up. Delilah came by our home I guess 5 five or six times looking for him and every time she came my brother was not available to her. She started calling his cellphone back to back. I asked him was it ok to turn his phone off? He replied yes.

Erical (Torin) I am going to get you a hotel room for as long as you need

Hotel was paid for a week, his daughter Tinesha and I visited when I got off work every day.

Torin (Erical) Hey I am calling to tell you my ride didn't show up today for work so I am back at the house. Hell I hated that I came back but I got to work. It was her cousin I was riding with but he didn't show up.

Erical (Torin) its ok, I understand. But I am here for you always.

Torin "I know"

"The mind heals much like the body does when it is wounded. It is a process and it takes time how much

28

time depends on the person. The scar never goes away and it becomes a reminder when you revisit it. Most people have scars on their bodies, we tend to forget how the insignificant ones happened but there is always that one you remember: when, where and why: it is still so vivid in your thoughts? Such are the scars we carry each day with our thought process...." (Adrian 2014)

I was standing outside enjoying an early afternoon in San Diego, and the weather as usual was perfect. The breeze was slight and the sun was shining, but it was just there as a prop. I decided to call my brother from my cellphone.

(Adrian) (Ring, ring, ring): Hello?

(Torin) (Sounds surprised but he replies in a happy tone): Hey, bro, what's happening?

(Adrian) I called to see how you're doing. Cita's murder has me struggling, and I just wanted to make sure you were okay.

(Torin) (His whole demeanor changes and I can hear his voice cracking): I'm doing okay.

(Adrian) Torin, come on, man. It's okay that you're not doing well, but you got to talk to someone. I've been in therapy since Christina passed, and as soon as I think things are getting somewhat back to normal another tragic event happens within our family. Torin, you have to pray. We know that God never puts more on us than we can bear, but he does push the envelope.

(Torin) I have prayed. It just hurts. She was a good mother. She didn't deserve for that to happen to her.

(Adrian) I understand and I miss her bad, too, brother, but right now, I'm concerned about you. I heard you're back with your wife. Are things getting better? Are you getting any therapeutic support?

Erical

(Torin) It's difficult right now. I don't have insurance for therapy. The sliding scale doctor I see for my medication only covers just that. Besides so much is going on in the home. Her oldest son just got out of prison and he's living here. Delilah doesn't want her other two sons living here, but you've seen how that goes.

(Adrian) Yeah, it's a revolving door with those two in and out of jail. How do you get any peace and rest with all that chaos?

(Torin) I don't. I don't feel safe in my own home, and it's difficult to live in this type of environment. Erical has been giving me a few suggestions on anxiety medications over the counter that would help me, and I take the over-the-counter sleeping pills just to help me get some type of rest for my insomnia. Sometimes I just can't get out of bed. It's not that I don't want to, but I don't have the energy or strength.

(Adrian) Torin, that's your system going through depression, and I know that because I was going through that myself. I would go to work and go straight to my room and shut the door. I was doing the same thing on my days off. I just wanted to suffer in silence. I didn't believe anyone could help me through what I was feeling. I definitely didn't want to talk about it. Look, I have to go, but I need you hear what I am about to say. If you need to talk, I need you to call me. Don't suffer in silence like I was doing. I love you. You're my only brother.

(Torin) I love you, too, and thanks for calling. I'll be all right.

It was the two-year anniversary of my wife's suicide, and I was preparing to walk out of the house to my scheduled therapy session when I received a text. It was from my brother at 5:08 P.M.

(Erical) Yes this day was an emotional day already for me struggling with knowing today was Chrissy's, two year suicide anniversary. My father had died with unresolved answers to his death. And then my sister just murdered by her estrange boyfriend. Enough is enough although God had other plans for this family. Honestly I felt I was being punished for something. I just can't get a break.

I worked so much to stay busy and not feel the hurt, covered the hurt with a smile. And cried in my patient's bathrooms and in my car.

I had just received a call from Delilah screaming in the phone: "I bought Torin some alcohol and a fifth of Liquor and I am at work... Erical (Delilah) why would you buy him alcohol? I get off at 10 tonight. She hung up on me.

When that text from my brother came through on my phone... It was strange on several levels. So I called my sister in GA to see if she received a message too. When she replied yes. I decided to call the local police to do a wellness check of his home first before I go over. They did and called me to say (Erical) your brother was not in the house. the door was unlocked and his cell phone is present left up on his dresser.. I said to the officer thank you maybe he just went to the store, I'll try him back in a few minutes.

I was just getting in my bed on the phone with my sister in GA and I could hear rushing police cars, Ambulance, lights flashing past heading toward to interstate. I said to my sister

Erical: It must have been a very bad accident on the highway. telling my sister to hold on because Delilah was on the other line.

Erical Hello?

10:00 pm Delilah "with a scream "HE IS DEAD!!!!! Torin is dead!!!!!! A car ran over him,

They're not sure. I got to go."

"She hung up." Erical "what, what happened", speaking to State Trooper Hill. Not sure what could have happened. Not sure if he was pushed, jumped .but I do know multiple cars have ran over him And because I am a Nurse this tore me up inside because what kind of human being would continue to drive over a body and not stop. Regardless if it is day or night I can tell if it is viable tissues and stop.

My brother was also afraid of heights so I couldn't wrap my head around him actually jumping into oncoming traffic he loved his children so much for that. What I was amazed at was how Delilah got to the scene of the accident 5 minutes after the police arrived when she was supposed to be at work at least thirty minutes away. And why would he want us to look after his hateful, abusive wife when she treated him and his children wrong.

, My brothers' death is still open and ruled suspicious. Closure would be when someone is picked up for due justice.

(Torin) (Text): "I'm sorry to all forgive me lord to my siblings please help my wife with this if u can and forgive me o lord. Sorry for me to be me. I love you all"

"For God so loved the world that he gave his only begotten Son, that whosoever believeth in him should not perish, but have everlasting life." (John 3:16)

(Adrian) (The text confused me and I responded): Torin, what is this? He didn't text back and I was running late for my appointment, so I figured I would get back with him afterward.

I remember sitting in my therapy session that day, saying to my therapist how it had been a long time since I had felt so good about life. It was going on seven months since the murder of my sister, and for my sister being my first and only sibling to pass it had been devastating.

(Adrian) (Speaking to my therapist): Thank you for everything. I will see you next week.

When I got home, I sat in my recliner and began to doze off. Therapy is draining, and even though it was a good day my body and mind felt tired. I heard my cellphone ringing, and when I answered the phone it was my brother-in-law.

(Adrian) Hello?

(James) Adrian?

(Adrian) Hey, what's up?

(James) Torin is dead.

(Adrian) Huh? What? Say that again?

(James) Your brother Torin is dead.

(Adrian) What happened?

(James) All we know right now is that he was struck by a vehicle on the freeway.

(Adrian) Thanks, James. I got to go....

I remember getting up and going to my room and taking three Xanax because it felt as though an elephant was standing on my chest.

I realized at that moment that my brother's emotional and mental capacity had deteriorated over the years due to being abused by two women who claimed to have loved him. The end result was evident that depression and alcoholism had eventually consumed his life and had caused him to jump off of a bridge into oncoming traffic on the freeway.

"Torin Demarcus Jones, I love you and I miss you. I knew you not just because you were my only brother but because you were my best friend. I was always proud of you, and I feel blessed to have told you that before you decided to go be with GOD." (Adrian)

-

Support Groups

- National Depressive & Manic-Depressive Association: www.ndmda.org; (800) 826-3632
- National Foundation for Depressive Illness, Inc.: www.depression.org; (800) 239-1265
- Dual Recovery Anonymous (DRA): www.dualrecovery.org; (888) 869-9230

- Alcohol Hotline: (800) 331-2900
- Al-Anon for Families of Alcoholics: (800) 344-2666
- Alcohol and Drug Helpline: (800) 821-4357
- Alcohol Treatment Referral Hotline: (800) 252-6465
- National Council on Alcoholism and Drug Dependence Hope line: (800) 622-2255
- Teen Help Adolescent Resources: (800) 840-5704

If you're suicidal, we recommend contacting the National Suicide Prevention Lifeline toll-free at 800-273-8255.

Chapter Three
Elijah

"Do not let your hearts be troubled. Trust in God; trust also in me. In my Father's house are many rooms; if it were not so, I would have told you. I am going there to prepare a place for you. And if I go and prepare a place for you, I will come back and take you to be with me that you also may be where I am." John 14:1-3

My parents, Elijah and Evelyn, raised six children. Two sons: Adrian and Torin. Four daughters: Denise, Erical, Velacita, and Anthea. I felt it necessary to allow the reader to see the side of my father that I rarely saw as the oldest son until I was in my forties. My sister Erica's story was touching to me because when my father raised me, it was all about church and work ethic. I would have loved for him to have said, "I love you, son."

The version below is her life story with our father.

Thank you, Erical.

Erical

My father was like my best friend all my life. My life growing up was, I guess, different than my other siblings of five in the same household, and for what reason, I don't know. All I know is I loved my father.

(Erical) I remember growing up in a prejudiced situation in fifth grade. I believe the teacher being mean to me.

(Elijah) Were you giving the teacher the right answers?

(Erical) Yes, sir.

(Elijah) I will come and sit in your class.

The next day, I was in class when there was a knock at the door. It was my father. He entered the room and sat in the back of the class.

(Teacher) (Asking questions)

I continued raising my hand, answering the questions when the teacher asked for responses.

When she called on me, none of my answers were ever right. They were either mispronounced or incorrect; however, the exact same answer that I gave was correct when it was given by another person of a different ethnicity (European).

Boy was this frustrating, and it was disturbing to my father....

He stood up and I remember hearing him say:

(Elijah) Maim, can I speak to you outside?

When they got out that door, all I heard was my dad yelling at her and telling her he was reporting her and that she would be transferred for this unacceptable behavior. I don't recall having any more problems with that particular teacher.

As I got older, my father would buy Volkswagens and I would help him glue the rugs down just to spend time and converse about everything.

(Elijah) I remember you asked questions about everything, but I gave up answering them when you asked me, "Why was the yellow Volkswagen yellow?" WE just laughed/

Going to church with Mom and Dad was never dull. Communion was always my favorite. Once it was over for the adults, my father would put the merita l bread in a bag and bring it to me with a smile. Growing up in the church helping my dad cut grass this is actually how I learned to drive a car by riding the lawn mower. "You can't go wrong and hit something out here." Anytime we had revival, we would still go even if we had homework. We would sit in the back and get it done. Dad was a hard worker at the plant making paper. The paper we all used to write on and the paper bags we all used to carry groceries. Dad was proud of what he did. I remember he gave me a tour of his building. His peers had great respect for him as well. I remember when Dad decided to go back to get his GED. Boy that was a great accomplishment for him. He was so proud. We took him out to Golden Corral, his favorite restaurant. Soon after that, he went on to get his certification for auto mechanics. So when it was time for Dad to get off from work at night, he would call Mom and ask if I was up and because he would bring a fish, chicken, or hot ham and cheese from Hardees and help me with my math homework. I was struggling a little in the eighth grade, but Dad tutored me. Dad taught me how to drive. Never did he raise his voice at me.

(Erical) (I remember one morning I overslept. Dad worked the 11-7 shift, so he was just coming home.): Dad, I need a ride to school

(Elijah) Get the keys and you can drive me to your school.

I was scared to death because it was the car from hell; it was the green "deuce deuce." That car reminded me of one of those long family dinner tables in a spooky house. The only difference was the table had wheels.

Well, I made it this far. Now I was dating a young man in high school, and my dad was partial to him. They seemed to connect pretty well. Now I was married and left home. My dad visited every other day for a while and would fall asleep on our sofa for a quick nap after just getting off from work most days, then early one Friday morning he was rushing over and passed my husband on the road.

(Elijah) Let Erical know that Evelyn was rushed to the hospital.

I left home with my house gown on and jeans with holes in them. When I got there, my dad was sitting in a corner with his head down, praying. Lord, right today tears still fall my eyes as I feel my hand holding my dad's hand. And I see my mom's face as clear as we are talking. She was an awesome mother.

(Erical) Dad, have they said what happened?

(Elijah) No, they just said she had a blackout at work and now they are running some tests.

(Doctor) (Shortly after I hear a voice.): Mr. Jones?

My dad stood up and he looked over at me.

(Elijah): Go see your mom. I'll stay right here and wait.

(Erical) As I went back to see her…

(Evelyn) Don't worry about me. I'll be all right. Take care of your dad. Make sure he eats right and takes his medicine. Go on home and I'll see you all Monday. They are just waiting for a room for me now.

(Erical) Okay, I am going to go out and get Daddy so he can come sit in here with you for a while.

Dad had eaten and taken his medication. And then he went back to see Mom for a brief moment. He said they needed to do some more tests on her, so he needed to leave. We sat and waited for them to find a room for Mom….

It felt like only minutes had passed when…

(Nurse) A loud voice from the opposite direction called out, Jones family!!

I turned to see where it was coming from. I saw a nurse, I saw a chaplain, and I saw a door. They wanted us to come in this room. As we came inside the room, my dad sat down and I sat beside him.

(Nurse) (Begins to utter those words): I'm sorry to tell you that Mrs. Jones didn't make it.

(Erical) I couldn't process what she was saying at all.... I need to see her.

We went down to the morgue, a cold room, as Mom lay along the wall with a white sheet over her.

(Erical) I remember telling them... She is cold. Can we please put a blanket over her?

I still see my dad's face at this time, staring at Mom in disbelief.

I asked my husband, James, to follow us as I drove my dad home.

When we got back to my father's home, he sat on the bed and tears just ran down his face. His heart was broken, and I felt helpless because I couldn't ease the pain. We talked about an autopsy, but he explained that because of his religion he was going to decline the procedure. My mom was gone at age 45.

Then a school bus pulled up, and tears fell again.

(Elijah) The kids, I didn't even think about the kids. How am I going to tell them?

(Erical) I'll try to tell them, Dad.

I met the girls at the school bus. They were ages ten and thirteen.

(Velacita) Girl, that's the best thing you could wear to come see us, a pair of jeans with holes at the knees.

Looking back in time, little did I know that would become a fad later in life?

(Anthea) They should never be worn again! Do you have to come out the house looking like that?

(Erical) Girls, let's take a walk. Mom was sick today, and they took her to the hospital.

(The Girls) Is she okay?

(Erical) No, she didn't make it. She died.

(Baby Sister Anthea) So what is a godmother?

After this conversation, the baby sister ended up shutting down vocally and responding by writing and the thirteen-year-old Velacita responded by lying and acting out.

When the funeral was over, it was just my dad alone raising two girls and working swing shift. I helped him as much as I could by going down in the mornings to cook, getting the girls' hair done, and making sure they got to school. Some days I would cook dinner to last for the week. Dad would sometimes come over and fall asleep at my house on the sofa from being so tired.

Then one day out of nowhere...

(Elijah) What do you think about me getting married?

(Erical) I don't think that's needed. I can take care of the girls and the house.

Before the week was out, my Aunt Jessie from Richmond called me. She was my mother's older sister.

(Erical) Hello?

(Aunt) Well, hello yourself, young lady. You and your husband pack a bag and come up here and spend a night.

And that we did. When we got there, my husband had pulled out the sofa bed in the family room upstairs; my aunt came downstairs.

(Aunt) James, come fix yourself a drink. Erical, I need you to come upstairs and talk to me.

Now mind you, my Aunt Jessie was never one to mince words. She said what she meant and she meant what she said. There was no gray area with her.

Our conversational began casually...

We talked about soap operas and bras and Charles Bronson's movies.

(Aunt) I talked to Elijah. He told me he talked to you about wanting to get married, and so what did you tell him?

(Erical) Aunt Jessie, I said Dad, you don't have to get married because I can take care of the girls, clean the house, and cook.

(Aunt) So you can do all those things, huh?

(Erical) Yes, Maim.

(Aunt) Well, can you sleep with him? Your dad is still young and he needs companionship, too. It's not that he doesn't love Evelyn anymore; he misses her but he needs someone to fill her void. Do you understand me, child?

(Erical) Yes, Maim.

(Aunt) Come here, child.

She wrapped her arms around me and held me tightly and she whispered in my ear, "It's going to be okay."

We went home the next day. I spoke to Dad and told him it was okay to do what he needed to do. My father married a lady; her name was Jezebel, and she had six children of her own. It felt like a real-life Brady Bunch family.

I never felt genuine heartfelt honesty from her side of the family. I guess because of the first-year anniversary dinner. I remember it was gift-giving time and his wife had opened one of the gifts received, which was a fur coat. Her family cheered and chuckled and clapped, and words of emotions spilled out: "Girl, we struck it rich, a nice job and money."

Boy did this set fire under my shoes. I was so heated, I didn't know what to do, but from that day on I've looked at them differently and I saw things so much clearer. I remember every year they had a huge family reunion down at my father's house. Those people never respected my father's house and property because if they did they would have never drank alcohol, played cards, smoked cigarettes, and cursed in his presence while playing that sinful music.

I felt disrespected for my father when I would come down there to visit because I felt it was not my home anymore. The siblings who lived in Virginia were made to feel as outsiders and visitors in the home we grew up in.

I remember calling down to my father's home to speak with him and…

(Jezebel) Hello?

(Erical) Hello, is my father home?

(Jezebel) He's sleeping now.

(Erical) Could you tell him that I called to speak to him, please?

(Jezebel) Erical, while I have you on the phone, could you please call before you come down to the house?

(Erical) (I didn't know how to respond. She was really telling me to call the house I grew up in, just to visit. Before I knew it, I had hung the phone up. Click….)

As years passed, nothing really changed as far as me getting closer to them. We still saw Daddy and her often. My husband had an injury settlement coming in….

(James/Erical) We sat down with Dad and asked him, how are your bills?

(Elijah) I'm struggling right now. I am the only income coming in.

While he spoke those words, it hurt knowing he was doing so much for her children and grandchildren. His pride was costing him financial freedom.

(James/Erical) We are here, and we have some money. You just need to let us know how we can help. It's not a problem; we love you. Dad, you need to finalize a will. We're just saying to think about it.

Dad thought about it and came back over the next day. He told us what he needed and he got it. This felt good to be able to take care of our dad like he has always been there for us. The topic of him taking care of his will faded and wasn't discussed that day.

The next day, James went out and bought a 1984 Grand Prix….

(James) Dad, I bought a new car. Well, it's not new but it's new to me. (Laughs.)

Dad came over with excitement, and just seeing the happiness on Daddy's face was enough for James. He went out and bought Daddy one, too. Dad loved his Grand Prix, and then her children needed a vehicle to drive and soon they took that over. I felt a different way when I found out that she never wanted my father's grandchildren down there. She wanted only hers. He would want us to ask her because then she'd say yes just so he could spend time with the kids. He would make up reasons to go out to Walmart to come by to visit me and the kids.

I remember the night Daddy called me...

(Elijah) We need to talk gather your sisters and brothers, see if they can come over to your house tonight. I'll be over around 7 P.M.

(Erical) Is everything okay?

(Elijah) I will explain it you all when I see you tonight. I love you.

(Erical) I love you, too.

Well, we all were there, except the oldest sister, so I recorded the conversation. Dad wanted his will and testament on record. We all sat there, and it was a difficult conversation and most painful for my brothers. They didn't understand why we wanted to talk about death. But eventually, they chimed in....

(Adrian) All I want is the suburban and a toolbox. The toolbox I want you to personally pick the tools because you made me work on those cars all the time.

They both laughed.

Although the will was not notarized on a legal document, I believe our father felt relieved to allow us to take part in a discussion should something happen to him.

Several years after this conversation happened, Dad was sent to John Randolph Medical Center via 911. I met him at the emergency room doors. Dad always said he never wanted to be intubated or stay alive if he had no quality of life and didn't know his children. Well, this night was different; I was not ready to let him go. Dad was breathing rapidly, tears running down his face. He was struggling to breathe....

(Doctor) Mr. Jones, we need to intubate you.

(Elijah) (He couldn't speak but he was shaking his head no).

(Erical) Dad, calm down, look at me. They need to intubate you by putting a tube in your throat so it can help you breathe. Once you start breathing on your own in a day or so, they will remove it. Is that all right?

Dad nodded and the doctors proceeded with the procedure to help my father breathe. I sat with my dad around the clock; even though he had a wife, he was my only dad.

When our father awoke, he wanted to write up his will request again with a notary and my baby sister who was home. We were writing when all of a sudden the wife from hell walked in and said...

(Jezebel) What's going on?

(Elijah) We'll finish that later.

Well, later that night, Dad called me...

(Elijah) Erical, that paper I wrote and that we talked about, tear it up. I'll do another one when I get out of here. She got upset and thought we were doing things behind her back.

So a will was never done this year.

Now it was tax season, and Dad and I sat outside on the steps, talking about life and how short it is, how his health was not in the greatest shape, and so he wanted to make sure his children and grandchildren were taken care of, and so I gave him $500.00 again to go see, Attorney at Law, and get the will finalized.

(Elijah) Every time I say to Jezebel we need to talk about my will and this house, she gets upset and says, "I don't want to talk about it now."

(Erical) I felt she knew his health was deteriorating and she was fine waiting it out. Dad, you do what you feel will make you happy. Don't stress and worry over this, okay?

Well, two years passed by and Dad was rushed to hospital. This time he didn't talk. He would write notes to me, and I would carry out his wishes. He did not want anything done surrounding his heart at John Randolph Medical Center. He wanted to be transferred to the Levinson Heart Hospital for his cauterization.

My father wanted to live…

I spoke to the heart specialist, and my father understood. He was transferred later that day.

Once we got to Chippenham Hospital, Dad shared with me of his fears….

(Elijah) Erical, I often have flashbacks on my mom and dad, my grandparents, and how they died from health problems surrounding the heart.

(Erical) Dad, you're strong and you're going to beat those odds against you.

"No weapon form against you shall prosper." Isaiah 54:17

Don't you want to be here for your grandkids? Don't you want to be here for Pooh? Don't you want to be here for me?

Tears came rushing like a raging flood…

Dad looked up at me and said…

(Elijah) Come here… (He holds my hand). We will talk tomorrow. Go home and print me up some information you want to share on the test the doctor is talking about doing, and we will talk tomorrow.

(Erical) (Kisses him on his forehead): Okay.

I went home with a knot in my stomach and water in my eyes. I just couldn't imagine my life without my dad. But I felt in my heart that he wanted to get the surgery or at least the pacemaker for himself.

The next morning when I went in to see Dad, he sat by the door and I sat on the sofa. He looked at me for a long time, and I knew. I felt his words before he said them. He pressed the button for the doctor to come into the room. We consulted together and Dad began to speak....

(Elijah) I thought about the surgery, and I am going to decline. I came in this world without any scars, and I will leave this gracious earth the same way.

(Doctor) Mr. Jones, can I at least give you a pacemaker? It will buy you some time to get back up here to me if something goes wrong. You may have only one year, if that, to get your affairs in order.

(Elijah) No, thank you. I will rely on the word of GOD, and I will exercise and walk and ride my bike and eat healthy and continue to take my medication on this borrowed year of life.

Oh, Lord, if this didn't hurt me to the core; it was at this time that I realized that my father's mortality was at risk.

(Erical) I remember graduating nursing school, and Daddy came to the school to pick me up. We went to eat brunch at Shoney's. It was great just spending time with my dad. From that day forward, Daddy and I were on the phone morning, evening, and nights. I could be in meetings but they had to wait. I would whisper on the phone, "Dad, are you okay?"

(Elijah) Yes, I just wanted to hear your voice.

We would talk for a spell and call each later.

Well, Dad stayed healthy for several years past the two years' mark. Ain't GOD good? Then one day—a Saturday, to be exact—I was home in bed around 8 A.M. I had my mother's gown on.

(Denice) Torin had a blood sugar attack and was sent to the hospital.

(Erical) Is Dad with him?

(Denice) No, Torin said he would tell Daddy later.

(Erical) No, if that was my child, I would want to know.

Denice called Dad's phone no answer, then we called Jezebel's phone....

(Jezebel) Hello?

(Denice) Do you know where my father is?

(Jezebel) He left out to go to the church to clean the pool.

The phone hung up....

(Erical) Denice, I'll run around there and tell Daddy.

(Denice) Okay, sis.

I dressed my autistic four-year-old, Pooh. Malik got into the car with us because all he wanted to do was help his granddad clean the pool. We drove less than a minute down the street to the church. Daddy's suburban was parked out front. I was sure he was at the church some, and the children began to knock on the doors and windows. The place was locked, and we couldn't get into the building.

(Pooh) Banging on the doors and shouting Granddaddy let me in I called my sister back....

(Erical) Denice, if Daddy needs me, I can't get to him. All the doors and windows are shut and locked.

Just as I said that, a blue pickup Ram truck rushed up and two men got out. They were walking very fast.

(Deacons) Did your dad call you, too?

(Erical) No, I'm concerned because there is no answer.

As they are opening the doors and walk into the church, they begin whispering and then they split up....

(Erical) Denice, they're whispering and I don't see Daddy.

(Sam) I'm sure he is okay, but please keep me on the phone until you find him.

(Erical) Okay, Denice.

It was as though time was standing still....

I walked around to the back of the pulpit, where the baptism pool was located, and I looked down and I saw my father lying face up in the pool. I jumped down into the pool....

(Erical) Denice, I got to call 911 for Dad!

I called 911 and immediately started CPR, knowing my dad was

47

already gone…. I asked, "Lord Jesus, help me!! Please, Lord, this is your child. Lord, give his life back to me!" "Daddy just breathe please for me"… I could smell the bleach throughout the church; it was so strong. The emergency medical technicians arrived and took over trying to revive my father.

My father was taken to the hospital, where they pronounced him dead. I went back there to see him and held his right hand forever and ever and ever. I rubbed Daddy's right arm up and down countless times. This felt so unreal, like a dream. He was my best friend.

(Nurse) Maim, we have to take his body to the medical examiner's office to do an autopsy for the cause of death because this is unknown. The autopsy will include a medical and toxicology report. Please go home and get some rest.

(James) Erical, Erical, come on, honey.

Well, my world was crushed from here on out. I was an emotional wreck. So as the days and stories unraveled, nothing was making sense. The detectives came over to my house shortly after my father's passing at the hospital and stated they did a walkthrough of the church and found no foul play. The church was reeking of bleach, and I knew the fumes from the chemical mixed with his heart condition were not a good combination. Now they wanted to search his suburban, which was still at the church. My cousin Kim drove me to the church so they could search it, and the detectives found that none of his medication was missing on that day from his seven-day medication container. The detectives then turned to me….

(Detectives) I am so deeply sorry for your loss, but I truly tell you, your father is smiling down on you and is very proud of you for putting the time and effort in trying to give him life back and not giving up on him. The emergency medical technicians said that when they got here to work on your dad, they knew he was being treated by a medical person.

I appreciated the compliment, but I felt so empty and the words were not going to bring my father back to me....

I drove Daddy's suburban home, and there it stayed. Later that night, the phone rang. My sister Denice was over and talked with Jezebel. Then I spoke to her and she said to me:

(Jezebel) Did the deacon leave or was he there when your father was lying in the pool?

(Erical) What do you mean?

(Jezebel) He said he slapped my father and asked him if he was sleeping, when he got no response than he went to get help.

(Erical) Lord, just hearing that hurt me.... Are you telling me that he left my daddy there needing air, breathing in all that toxic gas, and just walked away from my dad? What happened to the phone downstairs of the church, the phone at the store on the corner? Jezebel do you have Daddy's phone on you? She paused....

(Jezebel) Yes, it's around here somewhere. I will find it and call you in the morning.

The next day came, and we met Jezebel at the funeral home. This was the beginning of how she really felt about my father. It became all about claiming his possessions. His life with her was so superficial.

After the wake, at my weakest moment her family decided to come to my house and pick up my father's suburban. That said a lot about their character that night. My father's funeral was not as honored as he should have been; it was rushed and very disappointing.

Jezebel claimed all the insurance money and property and eventually bought a new home. A month later. She did leave behind their wedding plate, which all of my siblings signed and gave to them on their 18th anniversary. The wedding album was left behind. How could you love my father and leave those memories abandoned in the home?

My heart is saddened, and I weep in silence daily. He was my best friend. I still recall many of our conversations. I still go to his gravesite and tell him what he was wearing today depending on the weather. I would read newspapers and books out there by his side. I know it may sound crazy, but this is my way of coping today. I have my father's voice on tape, and I listen to him weekly.

Daddy's presence was such a positive impact on my family that the children are not saddened by his departure. They are overjoyed when we talk about him or go down to work on his home. Now that's LOVE.

(Adrian) While reading my sister's words, I realized that writing about her experience with our father was therapeutic for her. I understood there were words that she wanted to say to our father and for him. I'm happy she had the chance to share them with you.

Coping with loss is a process, and many times what works for one person may not work for someone else.

It is imperative that when someone close to you passes on that we allow ourselves to talk through it with someone. We must not suffer in silence. We must not self-medicate. We must persevere and press on. Our loved one wants us to be happy and live a fulfilling life.

The unyielding strength and support of our Higher Power is the answer to our suffering. I must admit that during my grieving and attempting to cope with so much loss in so little time, I have had my moments of such anger toward GOD. This for me is so conflicting because "I love him." I will expand more on this later.

It's been sixteen months since we started back to sharing our coping mechanisms. The truth is the healing process and addressing grief is a process. I would like to share our personal struggles. I felt it was important that sometimes we may believe others may be saying, "Just get over it and move on." In the past year, my family and I have experienced the following: suicidal thoughts and attempts, debilitating depression, loss of jobs, and admittance to residential treatment for depression, and suicidal thoughts and the potential of going to jail as an escape to remove self from life's reality. Isolation in my own home to keep myself safe. Masking tears because not everybody really don't want to know how you really feel. Unload on your psychiatric she is your real confidant. Making sure you stay on your medication is a big help.

God has been a conflicting part for me personally. I have always loved the Lord, but I have been angry with him. I mean, it was God who took my loving wife, father, sister, and brother all within less than two years. The way I felt was like this: Okay, God, what's next, my child?

I was able to write and publish my book called *Infamous* by Adrian "Ajax" Jones in June of 2015 by Dorrance Publishing Company. When the book was published in print, I felt no sense of accomplishment. I was grieving and had just been released from inpatient at a local hospital for attempted suicide.

It's difficult for someone who has not experienced loss to have empathy, but our friends and family want what's best for us. Don't push them away. Simply put, they are utilizing the only tools they have to reach out and support you. I say this because my wife, Christina, was in a state of debilitating depression. I mistook this for her just being an alcoholic. I didn't have the knowledge or tools to support her. I failed her. This was what I believed, and it hurt. My God, it hurt. I was ignorant to what was happening right in front of me.

The collaborating team who created this book to help us through a painful process wanted to allow you to see each of our family members' lives through a looking glass. Much like your loved ones, we want to continue to cherish any and all memories of them.

Murder is calculating, and there is no coming back. Our sister was a single mom who worked two three jobs in order to support her family. She was proud and did not hold her words. This story by Erical speaking of our sister Velacita is riveting.

Cita worked a lot when she became pregnant with her second child, Ronnie. I babysat for her on and off. But at that time, she was living with Ronnie's dad, KK, at that time. They seem to be a great team. My dad was into the boys' life, too. He was very supportive of Cita. Cita was very close to our deceased brother, Torin. They always took rides out to go fishing or just socially drive and live free. Cita went to school for her pharmacy tech, and then she graduated. It very hard for her to find a job in this field, which was very disappointing to her. She ended up doing janitorial work. Finally she went back to what she did best, and that's management. From management with McDonald's to Hardee's. She and K.K ended their road as a couple. She met a man named Rob. He was kind of strange in a way. She became pregnant with baby girl. She was so excited to have had a little girl. I was happy for her. Our father was so thrilled as well. Baby girl was close to her father, too. He loved baby girl with all his heart. Shortly after a few years went by, I remember receiving a phone call from Cita in the middle of the night. I can still hear her screaming in the phone, "He's gone! Bob (Rob) got shot!" I got my clothes on so fast and we drove over to her house, around the corner. Erical was there too within three minutes, we were there. She was distraught. All I could do was hug her and love on her as tears fell and soaked up Kleenex. Police cars were everywhere. Yellow tape surrounded the apartment complex and Bobby's car as his body was rested out on the ground. Bystanders were all out, and as always no one said a word, no one saw anything. "The ghetto...." That was all I kept thinking as police would come by people and ask, "Did you see anything? Did you hear any shots ring out?" And at that moment, I was feeling pissed and I remember telling folks then, "What the hell y'all out here for if your ass ain't seen nothing? Carry your ass back in the house if you ain't helping." Then I heard my husband whisper, "You can't be talking like that out here." Our father came over to help keep baby girl busy as I chatted with Cita for a while. She decided she was not going to stay at that apartment ever again and packed up and moved that night. Bob's killer was never found.

The day and life changes were decided upon and taken from our family home to uproar of sadness, confusion, unhappiness, loss, hurt, abandonment, and the struggle with forgiving on July 8, 2013 at 0800. The last day she was thirty-nine years old, the last day she told her son to come stand at the door while she got in her car for her last drive to work.

The memories of this day are embedded in my head as if the key was thrown away. You see, I have been trying to write this part of the truth for this book since Saturday and a stumbling block of something kept getting in the way of wanting me to stop or not reminisce of that day and the days after that.

Just a little insight on my beloved sister: Velacita Jones. Just these words alone cut so deep where tears just fall uncontrollably. My sister was a mom, friend, aunt, sibling, cousin, and somebody's manager at Hardee's in Hopewell, Virginia, as a dedicated worker. She had three children working and struggling to provide for them as a single mom. She did her best. I am a nurse at the nursing home down the street from her job. I pass her job every day going to work and every night going home. The events of July 8, 2013, tragically haunt me every day of my working life. As I get closer to the building, I think of that day and image the events: How many people could have been in there at this time? How many people actually saw the events occurred and did nothing? Were there a lot of cars in the parking lot like there are now? Every day I wonder that, and I don't know why it even matters....

What does matter that this man took it upon himself to decide on when my sister's life should end? God didn't have a say in this; the devil was very busy that day. Why couldn't he just walk away from the situation? My sister was growing up, had put on her big girl panties, and was living her life and broke up with this estranged boyfriend a month prior to his selfish act.

On this day, the worst kind of domestic violence reared its ugly head. He had some history in the military/police force and was still married but separated in question was all I was ever told about his life.

On July 8 2013, I drove past Hardee's. Her car was parked as she normally backed her car in at work. She worked faithfully daily like I do. So I saw her vehicle daily. As I passed, I said to myself, "She beat me to work this morning. I'll stop by and see her tonight after work." I got to work at 7:40 A.M. and went to my morning clinical meeting that started at 8:00 AM. At 8:05, my cell phone was ringing but I couldn't answer it. I just said I would call my sister Sam later when I got a break. Then shortly afterward, I received an overhead page for me. I took the company's phone in my office. When I answered it was my oldest sister Denice, calmly speaking, but I could sense and feel something was off and something was not right. She didn't normally call me in my workplace. She said, "Rica, is anyone with you?" Before she could tell me what was going on, I immediately got on my cell phone and called my house phone. No one answered, then I called my husband's cell phone and he answered. I said, "Are the kids okay?" He said, "Everyone is fine. Why do you ask?" I said, "Because Denice is on hold at my work phone and I feel like something is wrong." He responded with, "Well, go ahead, see what she wants. I will stay on the phone with you." Sam said, "Rica, where is Ms. Ruth? I wanted to talk to her." (Ms. Ruth was like family.) I passed the phone to Ms. Ruth. After they spoke for a couple minutes, she got up and stood beside me as she passed me the work phone back. Sam said, "Rica, I got a call a few minutes ago from Cita's phone. Someone said she was shot and she was going to the hospital. Rica, can you go over there and check on her and call me back, please?" I was frozen at that very moment, then I thought, wow, a robbery at the Hardee's. What a cruel world. Lord, I prayed she was okay as I was walking to go check on my sister. I wanted to inform my boss of this tragic incident so I could leave to run to the hospital. My coworker Ms. Ruth stated, "You go ahead. I'll stop by and tell her and catch up with you."

When I walked up the hill to the ER of JRMC, I was met by an officer, the hospital's chaplain, and a nurse who was standing there. I said, "Hello, I am Erical. I am here to visit my sister Velacita Jones. I was told she was shot this morning and just brought in here."

The nurse looked at me, and a doctor came over and said, "She had lost a lot of blood at the scene. We did CPR on her. I'm sorry, that was not enough. She didn't make it." "I want to see her," I said. "I'm sorry; the medical examiners have her body because this is an ongoing investigation. I can give you the police officers' names who are involved. Again, I am so sorry for your loss."

I couldn't scream, cry, or even be upset at that time. I could have been in shock. When I walked out those ER doors, the hospital chaplain was standing there and handed me his card as he offered spiritual support.

I must admit this was hard to swallow and understand as he was talking to me. Not sure all what he was saying at that time, I remember when my sister-in-law came in the hospital with Cita's three children. At the time they were twenty, eighteen, and six. They were quiet and, I could tell, very confused. I gave them a hug, and they asked if they could go see her. "Where did she get shot at? Why would someone want to shoot my mom?" the twenty-year-old asked. "She is the nicest mom. I hope she is not hurt." I quickly turned to them and said, "Mom was hurt bad and they have to assess her now for gunshots. We will see her when they finish." I just couldn't say those words "She is dead. She's not coming back to these children or to me." I took the children to the police station to get some answers. I walked the children down the hill holding baby girl hand, and I unlocked my car doors as they got in. "I'll be right back. I have to go inside. My job to get my bags. It's gonna be okay," all along knowing they would be traumatized for quite some time.

In Search of a Murderer

I took a deep breath as I went into the building with my coworker. We spoke to my boss outside, and then I was gone for over three weeks from work. We drove in silence to the police station, which was around the corner. I walked up to the window and spoke. "I am here to see the officer who is handling my sister's shooting." "You can have a seat, maim." We sat there for what seemed like it was an hour waiting, then finally an officer came out to greet me and I walked back there with him. He asked me questions of who I thought could have done this to her. I told him what I knew and that was it. She did not have any enemies. The officer reassured me that when they caught the person, they would call me ASAP. We left and went home. Family support was everywhere. All of my siblings were notified. My co-worker stepped in to find out what the children liked to eat, and she went home and came back with a full-course meal for them. My aunts came over to house sit with the children while I ran over to Velacita's house. You see, I got a call from my loud sister-in-law again, this time to tell me she was outside, across the street with Channel 12 News, standing there, watching somebody breaking in or break out of the house. Either which way, they were not supposed to be in my sister's house. I called the police to inform them of the theft, and they were gonna meet me there. So my uncle and husband rode with me over there because it was getting late. We decided to pack her house over the next few days. Right now let's just secure the windows and locks on the doors. The officers checked behind us to make sure they were secured. At 8 P.M. That night of July 8, 2013, the police officer called me and said they caught the killer and he was being arrested at this time. "You are safe. He will not be getting out." When they showed the man's face on the news, it hurt so badly because we invited this man into our home repeatedly and never saw signs of this behavior, and then again maybe those signs were there. He did not visit often when she came over. So on the news, it reported the man walked into Hardee's, gunned down his girlfriend, and then turned himself back to the VA hospital. I became confused on the story because I thought he was already in the hospital at the VA, so how did he get out of the VA hospital? Was he discharged or did he leave against medical advice? And last, how did he get his vehicle to do that to my sister? Because his vehicle, that green Escape, was in at Cita's house while he was in the hospital. And one of her children said that Cita called his wife to come by and pick his stuff up along with the Escape. She came with his son, who is also a police officer for the city. So again, if he is in the hospital, how can he get the vehicle? How was he able to keep a gun in his vehicle? I didn't know a person who was a felon could have gun in their possession. I spoke with the commonwealth attorney, and he asked that the children write how this murder and tragic event has impacted their life. Any other family members were also welcomed to write on her behalf. Personally I felt it should have been all of her siblings taking a stand for her, not that anyone's love was any less. It was more for support and to let this man know she had family and she was loved. So the first court date, he requested a bond and it was denied due to him having other drug charges pending in another court. His next court appearance, I did not have to show up for this one. The commonwealth attorney's victims and violence team leader called just to say court was pushed to 8/26/13. The trial began July 14 and July 15, 2014. They were hard to sit through at times while he lied about her character. And then listening to how he intentionally and maliciously intended to kill her and under no circumstances did he want anyone to save her. Okay, that was another large pill to swallow because that hurt knowing my sister lay out there gunned down by a man because she stood up for herself and he was a coward. And how brave those Hardee's coworkers were to try to help and risk their lives as well. Well, anyway… I spoke on the stand and looked directly at Green, and the newspaper wrote it up as: "Erical Tyler took the stand in July 2014 to speak on how life has changed since Green killed her sister a year ago. Tyler, who spoke through quiet sobs, said she now has custody of Jones' three children in addition to raising four of her own. After speaking about raising seven children, Tyler turned and looked right at Green. She told him that Jones' daughter asked her, 'Why did my Dad kill my mom? Why?' You don't even have a real answer for that." During the trial, the victims' witness impact statements were read out and the first one was by Velacita Jones' sister, Erical Tyler: "From the moment the phone rang for me at my job at work, on July 8, 2013, my world has never been the same. Tears fall from my eyes uncontrollably every waking hour of my day, every bathroom break, and every moment I am at my desk trying to do charts for my patients. I cry for so many reasons for the loss of my sister, whom I loved dearly, not only as my sister but as my friend. I cry for these children, her children. She has three children who all had special issues going on, and my sister was there for them and she loved them with unconditional love.

Let Go and Let God

The loss of my sister Velacita Jones has left an impact on so many people, family, and friends, but most of all, this cold, cowardly, selfish act of crime has left a lifetime scar on her three children. The first child, her oldest boy's name is Hank. He was twenty years old when his mother was murdered, taken away from him. He cried day in and day out, ate very little food, and lost weight. Hank did not come out his room much. He is mentally challenged on a second-grade level and can never live on his own, according to his psychiatrist. He is on medication to help him sleep with DX: PTSD, bipolar disorder, MR, speech impaired, and depression. Hank speaks highly of his mom, and I encourage him to continue to reminisce on his memories. Ronnie, her second son, was age eighteen when his mother was murdered and taken from him. He became angry within himself, holding a lot of emotions in. He blames himself for the actions this man created. Ronnie believes that if he told his mom to stay home she would be alive today. Although in the same breath, that awakening dream at night the thought occurs that if this man could create and cause harm in a busy breakfast place and gun her down, then would it have made it any different from coming to their home and shooting them all had she stayed home? This child was not sleeping well, having nightmares and crying at night. He is mentally challenged as well, as cannot take care of himself. He needs strict guidance to maintain functional abilities. He is on medication twice a day: for depression, MR, ADHD, bipolar disorder, insomnia, and PTSD.

Then there is baby girl, age six when her mother was murdered. She was quiet and very observant, never asking for anything. Her trust toward adults has been broken. She knows we love her, but she is a hurt little girl. She is going to second grade. She struggled last year in class with concentration, focus, and remembering words. She will wet her bed at times. She needs a sleep aid to get to natural sleep. You see, baby girls father was murdered when she was just three years old outside their home. And now she has no mommy. What a life to live with no substance of like mommy like daughter values to grow up with. She is clinically DX with clinical depression and PTSD.

Then there is me and my family impact: I have four children. One had just came home from college for break, one graduated high school and was starting college, one going to high school and college, and our last child is autistic with ADHD, silently grieving my father's death just six months ago while juggling everyday life. Our oldest child moved out, staying place to place with friends to give up his room for the middle child, who was still in school. And our college girl moved out to give up her room to her cousin Alexis. And our middle child's room was used for the two boys to share and have their own space but yet it is still so crowded. We can't take normal family trips, needing to drive two or three vehicles depending if all seven children are going. There are challenges every day. I was not ready for my children to leave home, and they were not prepared for the world, either. This tragic event pushed them out before they were ready to give their cousins a home. They sacrificed their stability as I struggled and worried daily then and now about my children because of the choices that were pushed upon us all.

The next victim impact statement was from my brother Adrian: "Your Honor, thank you for allowing me to address the court on behalf of my sister's untimely demise. My sister was second from the youngest of six siblings. She was the first of our six to leave us. So brutal and so inhumane was her death. She finally had enough and was leaving him. She finally got the courage to say to the emotional and mental abuse that this person caused not just to her but her children as well. This was the epitome of domestic violence at its very worst. My sister, she is a hero…. She was a hero to a lot of customers who were in that Hardee's that dreadful morning. You see, my sister took a volatile argument with this monster outside away from innocent bystanders in order to get them away from harm's way. My heart aches for my niece and nephews who have lost their mom and their friend. I called this act premeditated. He went there with a loaded gun. His frame of mind was if she was not going to be with him, then with no one. He deserves no leniency for this crime."

The partial impact statements of boys: Hakeem: "How I feel about my mom's death is it hurt me so bad when I heard it that someone told me my mom had passed away. A tear started down my eye. I asked God why he did this to my mom. Why he just couldn't walk away."

The Verdict

Well, now it was the final day for court, and Green had something to say to the courts. As he stood up with a piece of paper to read, he turned toward me to say, "I know of no words to console or comfort you. I am tormented, in great pain and anguish for this.... I pray for all of you to forgive me. I pray to God to forgive me.... I have fallen from grace.... I'm truly sorry, and I deeply regret any actions."

So this is how the justice system works. It is read several times to determine if this was a reason to rejoice or just know the struggle is real: Green is facing several charges, including first-degree murder, attempted murder, two charges of use of firearm in commission of a felony, and two counts firearm use by a convicted felon.

The verdict was in: The judge acknowledged Mr. Green's failing health and that he might not survive the sentence handed down. However, what has stuck with me the most was when he said the testimony from Ms. Jones' sister during this trial. "Mr. Green, you are sentenced to the maximum sentence the jurors could give you. And they will run consecutively. You are sentenced to thirty-seven years for first-degree murder of Velacita Jones, three years for use of a firearm in commission of murder, and three years for use of a firearm in a public place." When it was over, the officers and the jurors came over to give me what I felt were sincere hugs, although I felt in my heart this man should have and deserved so much more. Why can't people be penalized for telling lies on the stand and making up the lie as they go along? So many questions were left not answered when court was over. I feel my sister Velacita Monte Jones did not get the justice she deserved for a senseless crime. Not just from the man and the trigger and barrel of the gun but from the commonwealth attorney. I feel Hardee's should have had cameras in the restaurant to protect their employees. I feel Hardee's did not come through for her when her children needed the support from this tragedy on their property. These are just my feelings and opinions. These children never had a say in life of how their mom should leave them from a cowardly old man. A cowardly man with a weapon decided that for them, and now they live daily with the scars of July 8, 2013, the premeditated murder of their mother.

My friends, the hurt you feel is real. You and no one else cannot put a timeframe on your healing process.

However, today I am going to give you one assignment.

You have permission to cry.

I spent a lot of money on therapist and psychiatric help to help me heal, and the ten words of giving me permission to grieve, cry at any time of the day was free, and freedom of release has helped me begin my personal recovery of saying, "It's not okay but it will be."

I have to reiterate my confliction with the anger I felt toward GOD. I love my Higher Power. He has blessed me beyond measures, and yet these tragedies were his plan. He is omnipotent, and nothing is allowed unless he approves.

Last, we cannot minimize another's loss in comparison with our own. Whether it is a pet or homeless person they were helping. Life is precious. Cry, laugh, but of all things, live, my friends. If you take nothing else from *Save a Seat for me*, remember this: You will have good and bad days, and the good ones are far and few between them. Cherish those days because they will remind you of your greatness. I've learned to put in place a family member or friend for the bad ones when you just don't want to get out of bed or talk to anyone. Some journeys are meant to travel alone, but unfortunately depression isn't one of them.

Finally, share your story and know that you are not faking depression but more importantly, you're not alone someone asked me to define my depression. I couldn't. For me it is like being in a fog, struggling with hundreds of emotions and then not remembering the day before.

It's been a few years since the beginning this story of Erical and Adrian's struggle with complicated grief. A lot has changed with our lives. We both had to decide if we wanted to live and focus on dealing with our grief. Or possibly committing suicide ourselves because the grief was overwhelming. Complicated grief is dealing with multiple deaths and it is extremely difficult when grieving more than one person much less four people who were intricate in your family circle. Each member that you're grieving is competing for who is the most important to grieve and the mind can't handle but so much.

I believe it is important to share with you this experience that I had learned on my own. Everyone isn't equipped to support someone in grief. They may not relate to your experience and give you the impression to just get over it and move on. Or they may minimize your pain and grief, thus, leaving you feel guilty for grieving. I cannot re-enforce the important that those who are grieving must have a support system. These people won't hold you to a standard of grieving but will support you unconditionally in order for you to heal. Sometimes during grief there will be those that you have to walk away from in order fight for your life through the grieving period.

Thank you for allowing us to share our story.

CPSIA information can be obtained
at www.ICGtesting.com
Printed in the USA
BVHW081534240619
551821BV00017B/802/P